THE SPIRIT
OF A BEAR

THE SPIRIT OF A BEAR

Poems by
Kathryn Cloward

The Spirit of a Bear

© 2024 Kathryn Cloward
℗ 2024 Kandon Unlimited, Inc.
This book is published and distributed by
Kandon Unlimited, Inc.
All Rights Reserved

No part of this book may be used or reproduced
in any manner whatsoever without written consent
from Kandon Unlimited, Inc., except in the case of
brief quotations embodied in critical articles and
reviews with author credit clearly noted.

Library of Congress Number: 2023939160
ISBN 13: 978-1735957111
ISBN 10: 1735957119

Special thanks to Jennie Lapointe

_____

She helped me transform my life
Through unconditional love and her belief in me
She guides with patience and care
She's an earth angel named Jennie

"The doors to the world of the wild Self are few but precious.
If you have a deep scar, that is a door,
if you have an old, old story, that is a door.
If you love the sky and the water so much
you almost cannot bear it, that is a door.
If you yearn for a deeper life, a full life, a sane life,
that is a door."

Clarissa Pinkola Estes
Women Who Run With the Wolves

A Note from Kathryn

Through the years, writing has been my way of working through life experiences and processing what I am growing through. Most often, I am able to write in a song or in a poem the words that are hardest for me to express in a conversation. May these pages be a reminder that there's hope in struggle, liberation in pain, and personal peace in transformation. We are all invited to convert what is heavy and unspoken into whatever it is that makes us experience the freedom to shine our truest light. We are able to transcend challenges and use our stories for good. My hope is for everyone to experience soul-shining vibrancy and sustainable self-love.

THE SPIRIT OF A BEAR

Retrieval

It was a complete purge
Of the pain
She had to go back there
Once again
It wasn't to relive it all
No
She was there
To pick up the pieces
Of herself
That had been left behind
Her treasures of truth
Her gems of love
Remembering
In caverns
Safely
They had remained

She went back
For herself
Retrieval
In the pockets of her cloak
She filled with gatherings
Then blessed the pain
In gratitude
Leaving her wounding behind
Ready
She ventured back
Into daylight
Palming diamonds
To be gifted
Freely
Her priceless
Infinite love

At Ease

In their shadows
They smear her name
Stories full of lies
Fear casting blame

In her light
She stands and shines
Full of truth backed by proof
She has nothing to hide

They are scared
Worried frantic energy

She is at ease
Confident to just be

Weed

I've smoked weed only five times
In the last twenty-nine years
That includes the brownie I ate at a gathering
When I thought I was in the clear
But if I were to do a ten-step program
My introduction would be
Hello, I am codependent
In recovery
I don't know what it was
With men who love Mary Jane and me
Bongload-smokers who grew and sold weed illegally
Then in our ending, they'd blame me
One for over a decade
The other for a three-month season
While heartache clouded my awareness
Worthiness was the lesson loop reason
Yet through all of my therapy
And years of transparent self-discovery
I've come to realize it's never been about weed
My pain was their lack of truthful accountability

Perfect Wave

She's the one you wait for
The one you dreamed of
Every day
She's a chance in a lifetime
She's the perfect wave

Rolling in with confidence
She's unassuming
Ease and grace
Power surges naturally
She's the perfect wave

To catch her
You must be ready
Timing is everything
Paddling in to greet her
She's worth all the waiting

Many will never attempt
They aren't ready
To stand and be brave
But they'll always wonder
If she was their perfect wave

A Genuine Apology

I am sorry.

I know I hurt you.

I gossiped about things I had no business talking about.

I believed lies about you.
That version of you helped me feel better about myself.

I wasn't strong enough to defend you or speak up for you.

I perceived the situation all wrong.
I know differently now.

I understand you may not choose to forgive me.

I am aware of my wrongdoings.
I am making changes within myself.

Again, I am truly sorry.

Upside Down

Uncontained
Perfect chemistry
His every kiss
Activated me
All night long
Three times charmed
Then, waking up
In his arms
That romance spun
My heart around
He turned my world
Upside down

Lioness

She was tired of being falsely framed
By insecure hyenas throwing mud on her name
Manipulation is a cagey game
But a lioness can't be tamed

In her back every dagger she took
Because her cub saw the way she looked
Masking pain she carried on
Cut deep she remained strong

She defends with fierce loyalty
Against a pack, she stands courageously
She only rears up to fight
When provoked and when things aren't right

She's misunderstood
By those unwilling to see
A lioness is simply a woman
Loving wholeheartedly

Mirror

I forgive you
For all of the things
You did and said
When you didn't know
What you know now

I forgive you
For choosing less than
The highest good
For yourself and others
When you were unaware

I am proud of you
For doing the work necessary
For healing your wounds,
Releasing imprinted beliefs, and
Cleansing yourself of unhealthy patterns

I am proud of you
For clearing your vibration
To mindfully choose honesty
And integrity alignment
Above all else

I love you
Unconditionally
For all you've been,
All you are, and
All you are becoming

I love you
I am proud of you
I cherish and honor you
I am grateful you are alive
You matter

Allow Yourself

Allow yourself
As much time as you need
To process your pain
To sob and grieve

Allow yourself
As much time as you need
To seek healing
To feel relief

Allow yourself
As much time as you need
To rediscover joy
To experience inner peace

Joshua Tree

In the desert, we came to know
Silence is good for the soul
Winds of change blew through every boulder we climbed
We burned words of a past left behind
It took 25 years for us to find our way
Into the desert where silence had so much to say
We were once teenage girls with vibrant dreams
We fulfilled those
Then, started seeking different things
We were growing and changing
Accepting what was, what is, and what's meant to be
With children to raise and major life responsibilities
We were two soul sisters thirsty for change in Joshua Tree

Gaslit

They gaslit me
Into believing
It was my fault
For their
Cheating

What the hell
Where was my self-love
My worthiness
At the bottom of a dumpster
I guess

In business, I was fierce
In love, I felt weak
In time, it would be revealed
It was the covert narcissist wound
That needed to be healed

But until I was stronger
I took it and took it
Then one day, I finally said *enough*
Found a new place
Packed all of my stuff

That first night in an apartment
With my things cluttered on the floor
Dancing around, room to room I swayed
Relishing the new life
Renewed levels of self-love made

It felt so refreshing
To be free
Of the tethered weight I had allowed
It almost consumed me
Freedom, finally

The Spirit of a Bear

He's a humble man
With a heart wide open
Through acts of service
His love is spoken

He's an honorable man
With integrity beyond measure
Helping others grow and heal
Brings him great pleasure

He's a peaceful man
In the flow of compassion
Channeling kindness
He's a man of action

He's a healing man
With his medicine of understanding
Allowing tears of the wounded
A safe place for landing

He's a loving man
Heeding the call of his daughter
No journey's too far
For a caring father

He's a protective man
Holding strong with his care
A grounding force of nature
He's the spirit of a bear

Goddess Shift

We are raised in a society
Where men are amplified
And women suppressed
Systematically
To be told that God speaks
Through men supremely
Is the biggest narrative
Of misogyny

Selling us on a traditional family
Yes, that's the golden ticket
Saying our grandparents stayed together
Duh, women had no choice but to stay in it
That is until trailblazers marched
Carving our chance for new possibilities
Women organized for the opportunity to decide
For themselves, what desires they'd manifest into reality

When I realized I was on an endless treadmill
Stuck in the illusion but yearning to just be
I chose to be unpartnered
Sold my home and rented, debt-free
And to wrap a purple bow
Around this golden gift
Without fear of judgment
I offer up this Goddess shift

Through messages of love and compassion
May we listen and trust our inner knowing
As Spirit speaks goodness in all of us
But if it's not unifying, that's the ego playing
Aligned in love, this I know to be true
Without conditions, judgment, or superiority
Spirits love everyone as they are
Just as Spirit loves me, unconditionally

Burgundy Blood

It was a summer evening at dusk
Something felt wrong
Abdominal cramping
I collapsed in pain
Sudden moisture in my panties
Barely making it to the toilet
Seated in agony
Toes curled on tile flooring
Looked down to see
Burgundy blood
A color like never before
I knew what was happening
My body's rejection
Expelled from within
Tears poured down my face
Wiped
I hadn't told him yet
Now there was nothing to tell
Lost in a moment
I climbed into bed
Alone

Mega

Experienced the world
Enough to know
Every belief in being right
Is all about the ego
Teachings of
Moral superiority
The saved
The chosen mentality
It's all about mega control
Because being right
Is mega profitable

Curious

Curious questions
Masquerading as care
By slithering serpents
Seeking information to share
She knew better
Their spell she wasn't spinning
Coiled in their own false reality
Maintaining privacy was her winning

She Felt

She felt at peace
With herself
With her life

She felt complete
Without striving
For anything else

She felt content
With herself
With her life

She felt at ease
Without yearning
For anyone else

Only Four

I was only four
When you came and took what wasn't yours
Troubled by your past
My parents took you in offering peace at last
But how could they know
What you'd do when you got me alone
You told me not to tell
I guess I was a little girl who listened well

I stood at the door
Watched you run away happy there'd be no more
Myself I blamed
So I hid behind secrets and shame
Tucked it all away
In the back of my mind is where you'd stay
But how could I know
It would take years for those wounds to show

I altered my mind
That's when 20-year-old me would find
The hidden key
Unlocked a closet of frightening memories
But I turned around
Too scared to tell anyone what I found
I just walked away
If I avoided you I'd be okay

Yet time would reveal
There was too much pain to conceal
Even as I compartmentalized
Your imprint impacted every aspect of my life
Crumbled by remembering
Anger and sadness the truth would bring
And no one could deal
It was up to me to help my wounds heal

I chose the healing road
Through forgiveness, I released a heavy load
I learned to be okay
Time has strengthened me to not be afraid
There's no more shame on me
I no longer carry that energy
Now there's so much more room to dream
Like when I was only four

Wild Horse

I fell in love with a wild horse
A man created to roam and run free
Never one to be saddled or harnessed
Not even with the love of a woman like me

I hoped that I could one day tame him
But no matter how hard I tried
A wild horse can't be kept
He's not meant for a stable life

For a while, I took what I could get
It felt like enough at the time
But all I did was wait until
Sitting on the fence was no longer fine

Being disappointed by his nature
Was simply my mistake
Because loving a wild horse always brings
Excitement followed by heartache

I let him go
But the truth is
He was never mine to hold
A wild horse is no good for me, I know

Hummingbird Harmony

Flying in every direction
Serving to pollinate
Fluttering with light speed
Highest levels they vibrate
Wonders of creation
Joyfully playing in nature's beauty
Enlightening miracles of flight
Hummingbird wisdom is harmony

Was

I stood at the counter of the automotive shop.

As the attendant completed my transaction,
she slid the receipt across to me.

Then she asked, "Was Jack your dad?"

I stared at her for a moment.

Was.

Tears flooded my eyes.

Was lingered.

I quickly looked down and nodded,
as I signed my name.

Rushing my sunglasses into position,
I smiled as she expressed her condolences.

I could barely speak.
Whispered "Thank you" as I walked away.

By the time I opened my car door,
grief was pouring down my face.

There are a lot of firsts that happen
after someone passes.

That was my first *was*.

Unstoppable

They called her unstable
As she was treading
In an ocean of grief
Moving around in survival mode
She yearned for sanctuary and relief

Never did they offer her
A word of compassion
Casting judgments thinking she'd never hear
They called her unstable
When her eleven-year-old son was near

They say you're unstable, mama
He said from the backseat
Driving home after her birthday meal
An ah-ha moment she needed
Finally waking up to what was real

Deciding she'd no longer
Gaslight herself
Into silence on the high road
She reactivated herself
Into unapologetic self-love mode

Like a gymnast who wobbled
Balancing on a beam
She was never unstable
A survivor consistently providing
She was unstoppable

Golden Life

When I was in college
My brother's girlfriend told me
That when she was my age
She went on dates every night
Seeking only a guy to marry
Who could provide her
With the lifestyle she deserved
She encouraged me to do the same
My brows furrowed
My head tilted to the left in confusion
Was she for real
Oh yes, she was
Gold digging real
I knew I was nothing like her
And I knew I never would be
So off I went to fall in love
Manifesting the golden life
Of my dreams

Quiet

She isn't being quiet because she is scared
She is quiet because she is smart
She is strategic
She is savvy

She isn't being quiet because she is resentful
She is quiet because she is indifferent
She is protecting herself
She is honoring herself

She isn't being quiet because she doesn't know
She is quiet because she is wise
She is intuitive
She is in the flow

Crumbs

I didn't feel safe with you
Rightfully so
You weren't trustworthy
My guides let me know
Through subtle hints
Within my knowing
With pennies on my path
The butterflies kept showing
Soon I accepted and understood
I deserved so much more
Than the crumbs of love
I had settled for

They Only See

They only see
What they want to see
From the perspective of
What they believe
Being open
To different possibilities
Goes against
Their chosen reality
It's comfortable
Within like-minded community
A blurry lens
Provides clarity
They only see
What they need to see

Lighthouse

You don't have to move mountains
You don't have to compromise
All you've got to do is stand and shine

When they need help finding their way through
They'll make the choice it's not up to you
Because a lighthouse doesn't move

Let your light be the guide
Ripple love across dark skies
All you've got to do is stand and shine

You've done your work to heal
Your golden ladder revealed
Self-love is the key to shining

You've journeyed a long way
Through lessons day by day
Transforming, growing, and aligning

You never need to explain
Never, ever contain
All you've got to do is stand and shine

You're a lighthouse
You are strong and bright
You are here to shine

You're a lighthouse
You are love and light
Shine, shine, shine

Uncontained

Through pain
She grew her wings
With hope
She'd realize her wildest dreams
Uncontained
She could finally feel
Unconditional love
It's free and real

Unchanged

An angry (hurt) man
Blaming his ex-wife
Telling stories as a victim
She's responsible for their demise
It's easier to blame
Than be accountable for his part
Moving on to another quickly
Unchanged, again his patterns start

An angry (hurt) woman
Blaming her ex-spouse
Telling stories as a victim
He's responsible for their toxic house
It's easier to blame
Than be accountable for her part
Moving on to another quickly
Unchanged, again her patterns start

Being Me

I used to wear a mask that was molded carefully
To maintain an image of what everyone wanted me to be
For most of my life, it was all I knew
Until that day when there was nothing left to do
But take it off, it didn't serve me anymore
To play it safe, that's not what I'm here for
I started to live by just being me
Content with the treasures of my authenticity

It's been a long journey to find my way back to me
Removing the layers imprinted by society
Uncovering my truth, what's always been me within
And trusting what I feel with my intuition
I've let go of many things with courage and grace
I'm grateful for the lessons that got me to this place
Now I enjoy just being me
Wearing the skin of vulnerability

Beautiful Soul

Beautiful soul
You are seen
You are heard
You are worthy
You are loved
You are valued
You are deserving
Oh, beautiful soul

On Her Own

She did it
On her own
Not for a badge
Of Independence
Not to wave a flag
Of sovereignty
She did it
On her own
Because all she'd ever known
Was that she was
The only one
She could rely upon

Rainbow Goddess

Luminosity is your birthright
You are meant to shine
Turn up your power
Allow your true colors to align

Uncover your light from every shroud
Illuminate your natural vibrancy
Everything needed is already within you
You are unlimited renewable energy

You are a rainbow goddess of love
Rippling goodness naturally
Without effort or ego
You radiate Divine Femininity

Tease

They tease you and put you down
In front of other people
Oh, how small they feel inside
For it's from behind the laughter
At your expense
Their insecurities hide

She Flew

With stars in her eyes
There was nothing she couldn't do
With courage beyond fear
She flew

Little Girl

Little girl
We are okay now
We are safe
Healed
Whole
We did the work
Together
I am you
You are me
Within us
We have all we need

Fluidity

Like scales of justice
She balanced her alchemy
Aligned as one with love
Her feminine and masculine energy
Calibrated to simplicity and ease
Her natural essence is fluidity

Secret Keeper

Be a good little girl don't tell anyone
It'll be our little secret just me and you having fun
Hidden in my closet that's where he'd play
Why didn't anyone notice it was the middle of the day
So I held it all inside and cried on my own
There was no one I could tell I felt so alone

I'm a secret keeper I compartmentalize
I keep moving forward as I dry my eyes
I'm a secret keeper it's a lonely road
Hiding what is true is a heavy load

Thirty years later that little girl is me
I grew up to live the life, a script followed carefully
But all along the way over and over again
I found myself living the same pattern
Secrets I held for others and some I created
Deception and hiding are a lonely prison

I'm a secret keeper yearning to be free
The cry of my spirit needs trust and safety
I'm a secret keeper but I don't want to be
Will this ever go away I don't want it to define me

Healing and forgiveness gave me freedom at last
Secrets no longer harness me to my past
Then I met a man who wanted me to be
All for himself with love hidden in secrecy
It didn't feel right like a wool coat in summer's heat
I wouldn't be the secret he wanted me to keep

I'm not a secret keeper I won't compartmentalize
I'll keep moving forward even with tears in my eyes
I'm not a secret keeper it's a beautiful road
I'll never hide again what's not healthy to hold

I'm not a secret keeper I've set myself free
My spirit's finally soaring because I chose to love me
I'm not a secret keeper that little girl is me
We are living a simple life in peace and honesty

Honesty

In my darkness, I told many lies
With secrecy and pain, false words I hid behind

In the crumbling, light started to show
Now living what's true is comfort for my soul

There are no shadows in the mid-day sun
Open and receive love streaming from the magical One

Soul-shining joy is easy
When choosing to dwell in honesty

I was deceitful and I've been deceived
The price is high for what we don't want others to see

Cocooned through change as I healed my past
Now honesty provides me with peace at last

Warrior Woman

I am a warrior woman grounded and strong
Standing in my center arms stretched long
One arm reaches back to my past
The other onward to dreams I have

I'm a warrior woman confident and whole
In this moment present with it all
Knowing wisdom flows through me
As each breath aligns my energy

I am a warrior woman of mindful intention
Avoiding darkness with graceful deflection
My colorful light is a rainbow rippling
A journey of discovery for a soul's healing

I am a warrior woman I've got nothing to prove
Power within guides every fluid move
Peace is my weapon and love is my truth
Content with myself living as I choose

I am a warrior woman a crimson cloak protects me
Shaman wisdom gained honorably
My balanced alchemy unifies
A mindful observer with awakened eyes

Shining

She gave and gave
She complied
Their needs always
In the spotlight
While her needs
Unaware
Out of view
Out of mind

She gained weight
Shrouded emotional pain
Turned herself down
To dim
Reduced
Into their covert control
Busyness to avoid
Emptiness with him

In time, she admitted
She desperately needed help
Made the call
Activated her own healing
Removed the heaviness
Self-loved herself to wholeness
She reemerged
Shining

Muses

One was lightning
The other, pure magic
Musical men
With magnetic energy
Two muses of her
Vulnerability

Triangulation

They are the peak
Of every triangle
They create
Dividing sides
Pitting one
Against another
In every story
They are the hero
Or the victim
Depending on which
Serves them best
They can't help themselves
It's all they know
Triangulation
Nothing will change
Not in this lifetime
Why would it
Nothing is wrong
With them
They are the peak

She is Anonymous

She is anonymous
She has nothing to prove
She doesn't desire to be known
Her life's work is to plant
Words of change
Her seeds sown

She is anonymous
Through the years
Experience taught her well
No longer willing to take root
In poisoned soil
Her soul is not for sale

She is anonymous
She will leave behind
Harvest and seeds for new growth
As she's always known
To fulfill her mission
The message must matter most

Asking

Asking for what she needed…
She was nice
She was polite
She was pleasant

Nothing
Disregarded

She was patient

Asking again for what she needed…
She was extra nice
She was extra polite
She was extra pleasant

Nothing
Disregarded

She was extra patient, again and again

No longer willing to be disrespected
Asking for what she needed…
She spoke with a firm tone of voice
She spoke with a fiery tone of voice
She spoke with a fierce tone of voice

 "She's such a bitch."

Sigma

She is sigma
Feminine and fulfilled
Independent and introverted
Sensual and sensitive
Magnetic and mysterious
Loyal and loving
Bold and brave
Truthful and trusting
Disruptive and determined
Fierce and fluid
Mindful and mystical
Accepting and assertive
Confident and committed
Self-aware and self-loving
She is sigma

Cracks

There was a crack
In the living room foundation
Of the house
Bought it anyway

There was a crack
In the heirloom diamond
On her left hand
Wore it every day

There was a crack
In her pleading voice
Standing in the hallway
Gaslit, nothing to say

There was a crack
In the relationship bond
Of their marriage
Ignored it, busy at play

There was a crack
In her unattended spirit
Fake smiles and busyness
Hidden, never on display

There were cracks
In their splintered lives
Unbonded, space grew into divorce
To blame it on one thing is so cliche

New Moon

You put me on the shelf
He puts me above everything else
You'd always tell me not today
He says nothing baby is in our way
You shut me out easily
He's opened his world to be with me
You kept me hidden from your life
He's proud to have me by his side
You often chose to be selfish
He'd grant me my every wish
You'd say you're following my lead
He honors me with accountability
You held back and stood on the sidelines
He welcomes me in every time
You never saw the stars in my eyes
He says that I'm the brightest light in the sky
He's everything you wouldn't be
He'd do anything just to spend time with me
My world used to revolve around you
Now he's my new moon

Pay Attention

Pay attention and trust
It is all being done
With ease
The path forward
Is revealed
In synchronicities

Shadow Self

She walked with me today
We've become close
I am comfortable with her now
She used to scare me
I avoided her
I hid from her
I projected over her
Self-awareness provided acceptance
I grew to love her
Unconditionally
I stopped judging her
I forgave her
I released her from shame
I removed every chord of blame

We are aligned now
As one
We walk together
Write together
Dance together
Cry together
We experience life
Together
We are whole
I am her
She is me
Shadow self
Realization
Transformed everything

The Narcissist's Mind

Don't let them get comfortable
Telling lies about you
They'll never come clean
They'll never say what's true
Stand up for yourself
For justice and what is right
Scales are balanced when things are fair
And equalized

Don't be intimidated
By their bullying ways
Hoping you'll back down
Is the chance they take
Of course they're surrounded
By monkeys who believe
Every lie they tell
Because crowds contain insecurities

In the narcissist's mind
They are right all of the time
Deception and charm
Is how they survive
Taught to manipulate
False stories for others to buy
Lies are truth
In the narcissist's mind

Wisdom Well

I was at the bottom of a well
With wounded wings
He looked down at me and said
See, you can't do special things
You used to be vibrant
Now, you can't even fly
I'm the powerful one
You are weak in my eye

This made him feel good
To speak to me as if he knew
But that mole man had no idea
About the magical things I could do

In time I healed
Back together my wings grew
I fluttered my way out of that well
More whole and renewed
I didn't look back
I didn't need to see
For that well was full of wisdom
For a rainbow butterfly like me

Let's Stay

Weeds grew in our garden
With all of your lies
You didn't say what was true
I knew by your shifty eyes
But I stayed
And I watered our lawn
As the seeds of deception grew
We just carried on
Because I stayed
Yes, I stayed

I was afraid

You made me think that I was crazy
Tracking down the truth
I'd rage against my inner knowing
But the butterflies led me to proof
Then I knew
That I had a choice to make
And it wasn't going to be easy
The road I needed to take
So, I stayed
Yes, I stayed

I was afraid

There were many sleepless nights
Wrestling with my fear
When nothing was blooming
And nothing was clear
Then I saw myself
Through my little boy's eyes
And I knew we couldn't stay
Behind these walls of lies
We couldn't stay
No, we couldn't stay

I wasn't afraid

Now, my little boy and I
We're together living joyfully
In a two-bedroom apartment
We have sanctuary
One afternoon as we sat and played a game
He smiled when he looked up at me to say
Mama, let's stay
Yes, let's stay
I like it this way

Let's stay

Ripple Love

Walking around wounded
So many are in pain
Living within patterns
Of imprinting that remains

Shifting our perception
Expect miracles of change
We may all look different
But our hearts beat the same

We're all in this together
Connected divinely
The light shining within you
Shines within me

We all have a choice
In every moment we breathe
Let's choose to ripple love
Let peace be our energy

Uncaged

Back in the day
We would have been burned at the stake
Truth talking words
A witch's brew we'd make

That's how it would be shared
By those who needed to control
Keeping minds locked in a cage
To believe everything they're told

How long have stories been manipulated
Shaped by the voices of only a few
Who claimed virtuous living
Caged standards for what people should do

But our energy has cycled back
Again and again and again
To challenge the imprinted beliefs
Generations have been trapped in

Because it is a woman's womb
That brings new life forth
We're more powerful than they want us to believe
Uncaged we are a force

I Held His Hand

A plaid dress, knee-high white socks,
and shiny black Mary Jane shoes
A little girl full of wonder
on her first day of school

He held my hand as he walked by my side
He helped me feel brave with the courage to try
With a smile so wide he looked at me in my eyes
He said, *My baby girl you're my joy my pride*

An aisle of white flowers
and blue skies overlooking the bay
A celebration of love and hope
for a storybook wedding day

He held my hand as he walked by my side
He helped me feel cherished the day I was a bride
With a smile so wide he looked at me in my eyes
He said, *My baby girl you're my joy my pride*

Early morning on Thanksgiving
In a hospital delivery room
A crimson-haired baby was born
And a family tree grew

He held my hand as he sat by my side
He helped me feel worthy to guide my son through life
With a smile so wide he looked at me in my eyes
He said, *My baby girl he'll be your joy your pride*

His breath was getting weaker
But there was nothing left unsaid
We knew the moment was nearing fast
As he lay in a hospital bed

I held his hand as I sat by his side
I helped him feel at peace to move toward the light
As tears flooded my eyes he gazed at me one last time
And I said, *Daddy it's okay to go we'll be just fine*

Then, I held his hand as he journeyed to the other side

You Are Not Alone

I've got your back
You are not alone
I am here to help carry the load

Times have been tough
Pain runs deep
May my presence provide peace

We don't need to talk
Unless you want to
We don't have to process what you're going through

It's okay
To not know what you need
There's no roadmap for moving through grief

As a river flows
With gentle ease
As the leaves whistle in the twilight breeze

I will sit with you
Holding space
No advice no solutions just grace

You are not alone

High and Low

The greatest betrayals
I have experienced
Have been by women

While at the same time

The greatest healings
I have experienced
Have been by women

It has nothing to do with
Gender or gender identity

It has to do with
High and low
Vibrational energy

Phoenix Rising

She burned it all down
Ashes and flames
Her transmuted energy
Renewed without shame
No longer imbalanced
By unfair compromising
Transformation grew her wings
She is the phoenix rising

Free to Be Me

I was in a cage of circumstance
I'd never get to say, I'd never have the chance

I was conditioned with love as trade
Be what they wanted, give what they'd take

Sometimes I was their trophy
My shine brought them glory

But when I wasn't compliant
I was a problem to be silenced

I just wanted to fly
I just wanted to fly away and be free

Free to be me

Selah

Standing at the top
Of a Manzanita ridge
Gazing out over a rolling valley
Of lilac wildflowers
And ombre blades of grass
Swaying
With the wind
Selah

Sacred scenery
A well-traveled journey
For healing
Shedding
Transforming
Exploring
Becoming
Selah

A calming ease
Fulfilling breaths
Of sunshine's vitality
Listening
Knowing
Onward into the expanse
Of unlimited possibilities
Again

A Soft Place to Fall

Some days it's just too much for me
I reach my max capacity
When I can't seem to handle it all
That's when I need a soft place to fall

I can't tell you how hard it is for me
To say what I really need
When the tears crowd my eyes and silence calls
That's when I need a soft place to fall

Let me crawl into your arms and hide away
With your love, I feel safe
Crumbling my walls releasing it all
You're my soft place to fall

Miss You

Is this what over looks like
When all of the pictures get boxed away
And we go from lovers to strangers
I can't believe we turned out this way
I know I've got to let this go
I'm so sad but trying not to let it show
Being strong feels all wrong
When all I can do is miss you

My Dear Friend

You don't have to justify yourself
To anyone
About anything

Don't compromise your heart
For anyone
For anything

My dear friend
You are strong
Spread your wings

Let your life be your song

One Hundred Percent

They are one hundred percent
Committed
To misunderstanding you
Scapegoating you
Gossiping about you
So, why are you wasting
Even one moment
Of your precious life energy
Caring about their perception of you

Shift yourself into knowing…

You are one hundred percent
Worthy
Of being understood
Honored
Spoken about lovingly
So, why not focus
Every moment
Of your precious life energy
Caring about being self-loving you

We Never Even Kissed

I'm holding onto every word you said
Replaying memories in my head
I can never go back to how I used to be
Those moments with you changed me

You set the bar now nothing less
Will satisfy the thirst you quenched
To be alone is better for me
Than to settle for complacency

Now I know what pure magic feels like
When time stops and everything aligns
There's a calm force of intensity
With you, laser-focused clarity

I cannot undo this
Leveled up awareness
Transformed absolute bliss
And we never even kissed

Thank Goodness

Looking back
At all of the years
Self-doubting
 Shape-shifting
  Light-dimming
    Career-striving
      Drama-spinning
       People-pleasing
         Energy-depleting
           Fulfillment-seeking
She thought to herself
Thank goodness, all of that is behind me now!

Trinity

Mother Nature watered my garden with love
Father Time steadied my mind with patience
Great Spirit infused my soul with wisdom

Karli

By the fountain in the park
They danced to the music as it got dark
Those summer nights spent with Karli
A dad's joy held in his memory

Forever touched never the same
Karli was mighty in spirit, a deep-hearted flame
Knowing our words have energy
She left pieces of love in anyone she'd meet

Karli loved animals and rescued every stray on the street
With her mom, their company made healthy animal treats
The future was bright with so much going her way
Then everything changed that January day

Karli had been dealing with anxiety
Bought a pill on the street because it was cheap
She took it hoping for some relief
Then her parents woke to a call no one wants to receive

Laced with Fentanyl, Karli's body had given in
Overdosed on a drug she had no idea she'd taken
Fentanyl has taken far too many lives
There's more to Karli's story than how she died

Answering the Call

Some don't understand
But it's not in their hands
Our knowing is to trust
Goodness guides us
To answer the call of our souls
Detached we let go
Allowing ourselves to be guided
Trusting all is provided
Surrendering our will
Divine flow is our fill
Actions without ego's control
Answering the call of our souls

His Love

I don't have a template for this
A man treating me like a goddess
Rose petals on the ground
My heart was finally safe and sound

I know my angels brought him to me
I'd been praying for a man of integrity
A gentleman through and through
There's nothing he wouldn't do

His love revitalized me
His strength was nurturing
He listened with tenderness
His love was bliss

In Time

She felt shame
She took the blame
She remained quiet

False stories were told
Lies embedded in the fold
She remained quiet

She turned herself to dim
Struggled to find love from within
She remained quiet

In time…

She healed and grew
With wings of awareness, she flew
Her voice rediscovered

Knowing she had nothing to prove
Protected in divine truth
Her light uncovered

Content with ease and simplicity
Her words wove a colorful tapestry
Her power recovered

In the Deep

In the deep
Down under
Is where you'll find her
Like the ocean
Her interior world is self-contained
An expansive ecosystem of vitality
Intentional interconnectivity

Alert and aware
In the deep
Down under
Exploring and adventuring
New realms of curiosity
She is pure
Natural

Selection
For unearthing
Aspects of herself
To be surfaced
A sacred process
Her priceless treasures
Revealed

Depth diving
Feels safe
She is free
So much of her
Remains forever
In the deep
Down under

Poetry in Songs

Thank you for reading my poetry. Some of the poems in this book are also shared as lyrics in my songs as listed below. I invite you to listen and feel the lyrical poetry shared through my music at KathrynClowardMusic.com and all music sites.

Lioness (from "She Roared")
Wild Horse
Lighthouse
Being Me
She Flew
Secret Keeper
Honesty
Warrior Woman
New Moon
Let's Stay
Ripple Love
I Held His Hand
You Are Not Alone
Free to Be Me
A Soft Place to Fall
Miss You
My Dear Friend (from "She Flew")
We Never Even Kissed
Answering the Call

About Kathryn

Kathryn Cloward is an award-winning songwriter-artist, author, and poet. Known as "Kathryn the Grape" to children, she's a prolific storyteller who crafts complex topics into simplified stories and songs for all ages. Through her unmasked and authentic songwriting and poetry for teen and adult audiences, Kathryn reveals the introspective and passionate woman she is and her continuous journey of transformative self-love. KathrynCloward.com

Request for Reviews

If you feel inclined to do so, kindly share a review for "The Spirit of a Bear" on Amazon or Goodreads. The QR code for Amazon is below. Simply scan it with your phone or tablet to be directed to the book's page.

www.ingramcontent.com/pod-product-compliance
Lightning Source LLC
Chambersburg PA
CBHW021117080526
44587CB00010B/549